Top 10 Worst Things about Ancient Greece you wouldn't want to know!

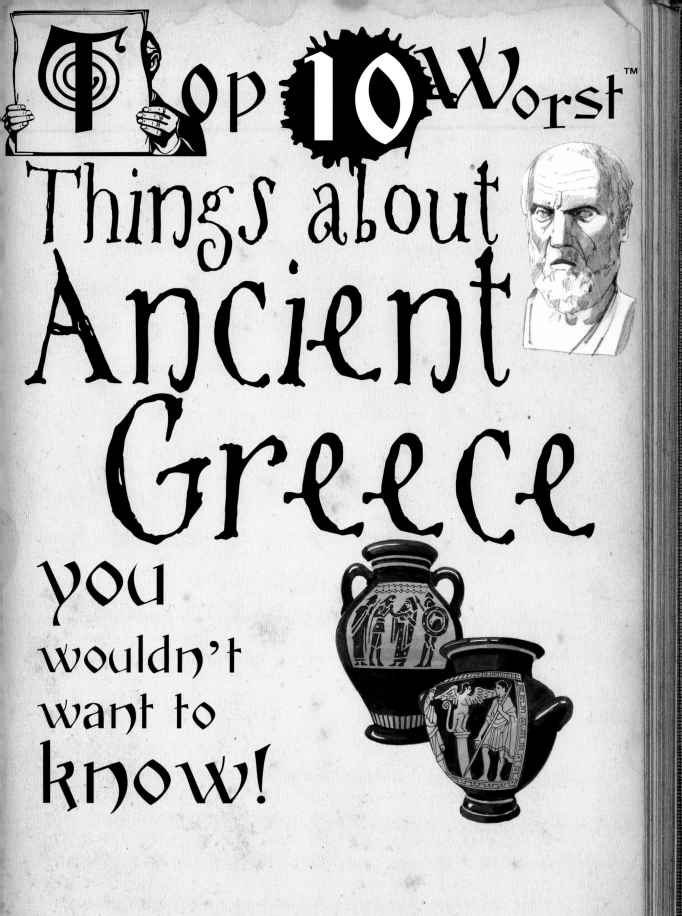

Gareth Stevens
Publishing

Please visit our Web site, **www.garethstevens.com**. For a free color catalog of all our high-quality books, call toll free 1-800-542-2595 or fax 1-877-542-2596.

Library of Congress Cataloging-in-Publication Data

England, Victoria.
Top 10 worst things about Ancient Greece / Victoria England.
p. cm. — (Top 10 worst)
Includes index.
ISBN 978-1-4339-6692-7 (pbk.)
ISBN 978-1-4339-6693-4 (6-pack)
ISBN 978-1-4339-6691-0 (library binding)
1. Greece—Civilization—To 146 B.C.—Juvenile literature. I. Title. II. Title:
Top ten worst things about Ancient Greece.
DF77.E54 2012
938—dc23

2011016314

First Edition

Published in 2012 by
Gareth Stevens Publishing
111 East 14th Street, Suite 349
New York, NY 10003

© 2012 The Salariya Book Company Ltd

Series creator: David Salariya
Editor: Victoria England
Illustrations by David Antram

All rights reserved. No part of this book may be reproduced in any form without permission from the publisher, except by reviewer.

Printed in Heshan, China

CPSIA compliance information: Batch #SW12GS:
For further information contact
Gareth Stevens, New York,
New York at 1-800-542-2595.

Top 10 Worst

Things about Ancient Greece

you wouldn't want to know!

Illustrated by
David Antram

Written by
Victoria England

Created & designed by
David Salariya

Contents

Where in the world? 5

Life in ancient Greece 6

Daily life for the ancient Greeks 8

No. 10: food and drink 10

No. 9: family life and education 12

No. 8: Medicine and healing miracles 14

No. 7: Down on the farm 16

No. 6: Home comforts 18

No. 5: Travel and transport 20

No. 4: Politics and voting 22

No. 3: The Olympic Games 24

No. 2: Spartans at war 26

No. 1: Life as a slave 28

Glossary 30

Index 32

Where in the world?

Situated at the eastern end of the Mediterranean Sea is the land of Greece. It is a rugged place, with mountains covering almost three-quarters of the land. The civilization of the ancient Greeks was at its most glorious between about 500 BC and 300 BC. For the most part, Greece was a prosperous and beautiful place to live, but what were the worst things about living as an ancient Greek?

Life in ancient Greece

Ancient Greece was beautiful, but it was also harsh. Summers were very hot, but winters brought icy winds and driving rain. Disease, shipwreck, earthquakes, war (for men), and childbirth (for women) killed many. That is why Greek men and women said prayers and offered sacrifices to so many gods and goddesses.

Greek religion

The most important gods were a family of twelve Olympians, said to live on Mount Olympus, a mountain that seemed to reach up to heaven itself. They were worshipped throughout the Greek world and temples were built in their honor.

Zeus

Hera

Demeter

Hermes

Poseidon

Dionysus

Artemis

Aphrodite

Apollo

Ares

Athena

Hephaestus

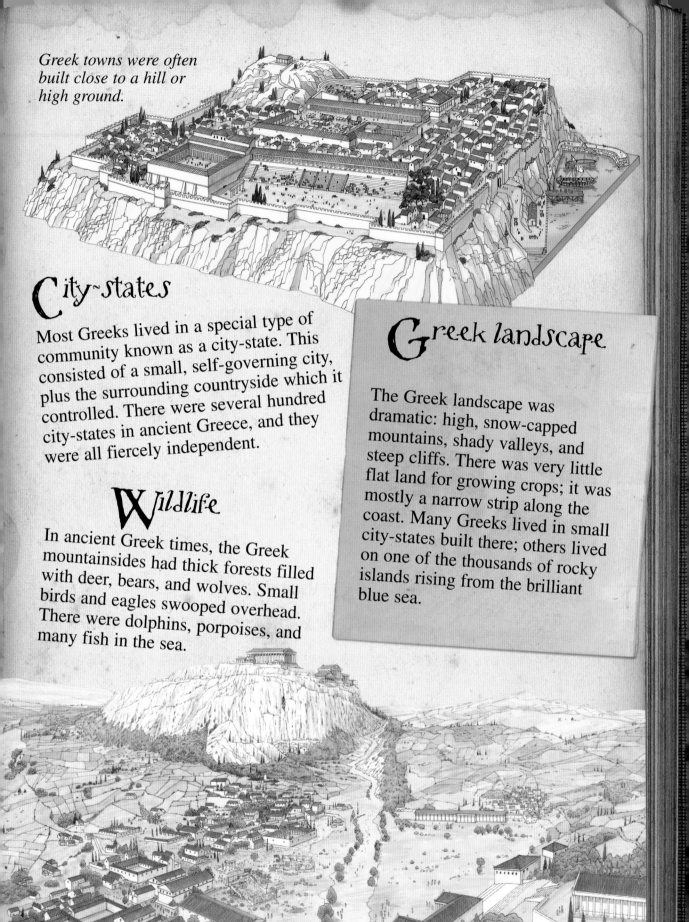

Greek towns were often built close to a hill or high ground.

City-states

Most Greeks lived in a special type of community known as a city-state. This consisted of a small, self-governing city, plus the surrounding countryside which it controlled. There were several hundred city-states in ancient Greece, and they were all fiercely independent.

Wildlife

In ancient Greek times, the Greek mountainsides had thick forests filled with deer, bears, and wolves. Small birds and eagles swooped overhead. There were dolphins, porpoises, and many fish in the sea.

Greek landscape

The Greek landscape was dramatic: high, snow-capped mountains, shady valleys, and steep cliffs. There was very little flat land for growing crops; it was mostly a narrow strip along the coast. Many Greeks lived in small city-states built there; others lived on one of the thousands of rocky islands rising from the brilliant blue sea.

Daily life for the ancient Greeks

A woman's world

Scrubbing the floors took the slaves hours each day.

Greek women were valued for what they did for others, like being faithful to their husbands and creating a comfortable home, not for what they did to fulfill themselves. As wives, their most important task was to give birth to children, to continue their husband's family. The wives of rich citizens and farmers mostly stayed at home and couldn't take part in public life.

Getting an education

Greeks who could afford it valued learning very highly; boys were sent to study at school, while girls were taught at home. Even ordinary citizens enjoyed plays and stories written by world-class poets. Many people still admire them today.

Schoolboys learned how to read and write, how to calculate using an abacus, and how to sing and recite poetry.

Language and letters

To the ancient Greeks, all strangers were "barbarians." They were uncivilized, because they did not speak Greek. For many centuries, the Greek language had not been written down; poems and songs had been memorized and passed on by word of mouth. But, long before the 5th century BC, Greek scribes devised an alphabet of letters and sounds from the earlier Phoenician language. It is still used today.

Athenian potters used two different painting techniques. Black-figure pottery was produced first and red-figure pottery was produced later.

Arts and crafts

Museums today often include examples of ancient Greek pottery. It was made of smooth, fine, red clay, painted with dramatic patterns or lively scenes. We know about Greek pottery because a lot of it has survived. But many other skillful Greek craftworkers, jewelers, metalworkers, weavers, sculptors, and carpenters produced goods to the same high standard, as well as simpler everyday items.

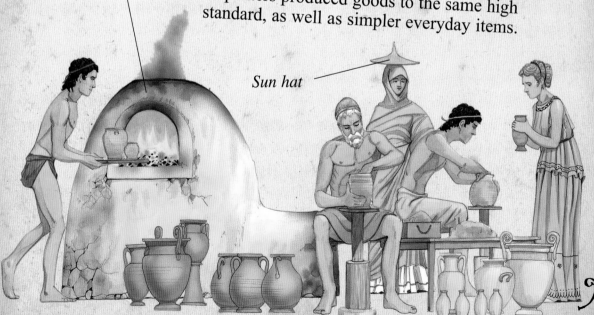

Kiln

Sun hat

No 10

food and drink

She was needing a bath!

Splash!

ood in ancient Greece was very simple: bread, milk, beans, olives, grapes, figs, and, in summer, fresh vegetables and herbs. However, as the population grew, famine was always a possibility. And in wartime, armies set fire to crops in the fields, trying to starve their enemies into surrender.

Water & wine

All drinking water had to be carried, usually by women, from wells or from mountain springs. Wine was carried in sewn-up goatskins, which were transported by donkey or mule.

For rich people, one of their favorite ways of spending an evening would be relaxing with their friends at a "symposium" or dinner party.

Be prepared!
Always expect the very worst

Imports and exports

Merchants sailed from port to port, buying and selling goods:

- Wheat to make bread was imported from lands north of the Black Sea.

- Salted fish was sent from the Greek islands to cities on the mainland.

- Greek olive oil was exported throughout the lands around the Mediterranean.

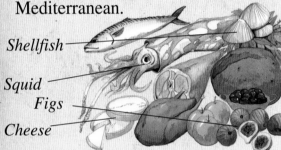

Shellfish
Squid
Figs
Cheese

The grain trade

Many of the Greek cities could not grow enough to feed all their people, so grain—mainly barley—was the most crucial import. Athens had to import as much as two-thirds of all its grain from abroad, mostly from Greek colonies around the shores of the Black Sea.

Greek ship

Agora (marketplace)

How to play kottabos

Kottabos* was a favorite game played at men's dinner parties.

- First, drink lots of wine. Drunkenness was allowed at parties like these.

- Leave a little wine in the bottom of a drinking cup. A wide cup makes the game more difficult; it is more awkward to handle than a narrow one.

- Fix a target on the wall or put a pot on a stand. Fling your wine at it, calling out your wife's name. The person whose wine lands nearest the target is the most faithful husband.

Drink wine

Leave some in cup

Throw at target

Don't try this at home!

11

No 9

family life and education

Families worshipped together, but they were not all equal. Men were in charge. They protected and provided for women and children, but they also controlled them. In most Greek states women could not own property, and always had to be under the legal guardianship of a man—a husband, father, or other male relative.

Marriage ceremonies were held in the home of the bride's father, but the bride herself did not have to be present.

It's a man's world

Family was very important for the ancient Greeks and often included slaves and servants living in the home. They, too, were the father's responsibility. He could send children away to be adopted, divorce his wife, or even marry her to someone else against her will.

Mothers stopped looking after their sons at the age of six, when their fathers took charge.

Be prepared!
Always expect the very worst

Life for a girl

Girls were not allowed to leave home or go to school. Their education would include traditional female skills, like spinning and weaving, as well as learning to read, write, and calculate. The father even decided who his daughter would marry.

Stylus

Wax tablet

Subjects at school

- Writing was an important part of education. Children were taught to inscribe letters on wax tablets with a stylus.

- Children were taught arithmetic by counting beads on an abacus.

Abacus

School for boys

The teachers at school were strict and the main part of a child's education revolved around Greek history, which included learning vast amounts of philosophy and poetry by heart. Greek teachers aimed at producing a well-balanced individual, with a "healthy mind in a healthy body," so sport was just as important as the other lessons.

- A stringed instrument called a lyre was often used to accompany poetry recitals.

Lyre

13

No 8

Medicine and healing miracles

The ancient Greek philosophers began to ask challenging questions like "What was the origin of life?" or "If horses could draw, how would they portray their gods?" At the same time, scientists were making great discoveries about "natural laws" in mathematics, music, and medicine. However, many scientists and philosophers were regarded as dangerous revolutionaries by citizens and their rulers.

Surgical instruments

Surgical instruments were made of bronze and iron. They included forceps, knives, and probes. With these, doctors operated on different parts of the body, using opium and the root of the mandrake (a powerful herb) as anesthetics. These were not very effective and operations must have been painful and very dangerous!

Hippocrates of Cos

In the 5th century BC, Hippocrates of Cos, the "father of medicine," ran a training school for doctors. His students swore a solemn oath to live "pure and holy lives" and to put their patients' welfare first. The rules of good medical practice that Hippocrates laid down still guide doctors today.

14

Be prepared!
Always expect the very worst

Going to the doctor

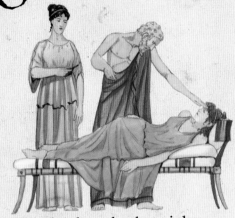

The Greeks thought that sickness and disease were punishments sent by the gods, so they asked the gods to help cure them. They particularly went to the god of medicine, Asclepios. His most famous temple was at Epidaurus, where sick people went in large numbers.

Healing miracles

At the temple of Epidaurus, the healer god Asclepios was believed to visit sick people in their dreams.

They heard stories from the temple priests.

One tale told of Asclepios touching a man's hand as he slept. When he awoke, he was cured.

Worshippers were told to leave gifts for Asclepios. Only then would he be able to cure them. Sight could be restored by giving a gift of silver.

Thanks offerings

Patients often used terra-cotta or bronze models to show which part of their body was injured or sick. Patients who had been cured by their overnight stay at a temple hospital gave offerings of thanks called *ex-votos* in the shape of the body parts which had been healed.

No 9

Down on the farm

Working on a farm was hard. The weather was harsh, the soil was stony, and farmers had to pay a hefty tax to the government. There were also few machines to help—only an ox-drawn plow and simple wooden presses. Even the smallest farm had at least one slave, and large farms had dozens.

Slave labor

Slaves did all the hard work preparing the soil, planting and harvesting the crops, and storing them for winter use. They also cared for the animals, made olive oil, wine, and cheese, and gathered wild foods.

Be prepared!
Always expect the very worst

The farming year

- **LATE SPRING:** Help with haymaking.

- **SUMMER:** Use sticks to beat the olive trees so fruit falls to the ground.

- **AUTUMN:** Gather berries, nuts, and mushrooms from the forest.

- **WINTER:** Look at the cheeses made earlier in the year. Are they maturing, or full of maggots?

- **EARLY SPRING:** Look after the newborn animals. They're always hungry!

Grape harvest

The grape harvest was a busy time. Each bunch of grapes was picked by hand, then carried in sticky, oozy baskets to the farmyard, where they were left for 9 days and then crushed to extract their juice. This was left to ferment and turn into wine. At first, squashing the grapes was fun, but in the heat of the sun, crushers soon got tired.

Pressing the olives

Slaves had to be very strong to work the olive press. Ripe green olives were packed into nets, then crushed between two heavy stones using a huge, weighted wooden lever. The oil from the olives was used for cooking and to preserve food. Low-grade oil was burned in little lamps, and used to clean and soften the skin.

No 6

Home comforts

Originally, most Greek people lived and worked in the countryside. But after around 700 BC, towns grew bigger and poor farmers and their servants migrated there. Everywhere, the streets seemed full of people, from proud rich men with bodyguards to beggars in the dirt.

A craftworker's house

Craftworkers in the town lived in houses like this. It would have been one in a block of homes for 10 families. The house is built around a courtyard, containing the family altar where you make offerings to the gods. It is shielded from the street by a strong gate and a high wall.

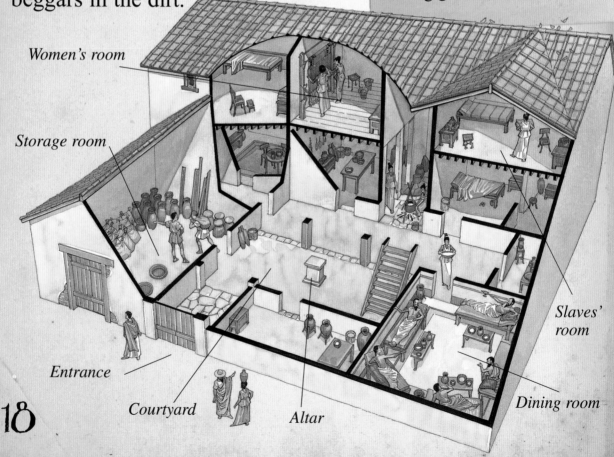

Women's room

Storage room

Entrance

Courtyard

Altar

Slaves' room

Dining room

Be prepared!
Always expect the very worst

On the streets

The air was noisy with the hammering, shouting and clatter of horses' hooves. It was also very smelly; there were no sewers. At night, servants with torches escorted groups of partygoers and kept a lookout for thieves.

Household chores

Household slaves called *oiketai* were needed to do the daily tasks. They did all the cooking, cleaning, lighting of fires, and collecting loads of heavy firewood.

Puff!

Living in a town

Towns were also home to slaves and other non-citizens: traveling merchants, craftsmen, scholars, and sailors. Overcrowding—and disputes about town government—sometimes led to problems. Athens (population 250,000) faced famine, plague, bitter political rivalry, and slave revolts.

Slaves were at the beck and call of their owner's wives. They would be scolded if she wasn't happy with their work.

Stupid slave girl!

Who'd be a slave?

No 5

Travel and transport

The best way to explore a world beyond Greece was to travel by sea, sailing from island to island or along the coast. However, Greek sailors did not like to venture far out of sight of land. They had no compasses to help them steer or fix their positions, and had to rely on the stars. Winter storms made the seas dangerous; many ships were wrecked.

The earliest Greek ships were fairly small (maybe 30 m long) with one bank of oars and a simple sail.

Sea transport

Transport by sea was often quicker than by land. Ships could carry far greater loads than wagons. They brought stone, especially marble, from the Greek islands.

But sea transport had its dangers. Many valuable loads of stone ended up at the bottom of the sea when ships sailed onto rocks or were overcome by storms.

Be prepared!
Always expect the very worst

Bumpy roads

Poor roads with potholes and rough surfaces sometimes caused accidents to happen. Wheels came off wagons and oxen lost their footing and fell!

A   B   C

D

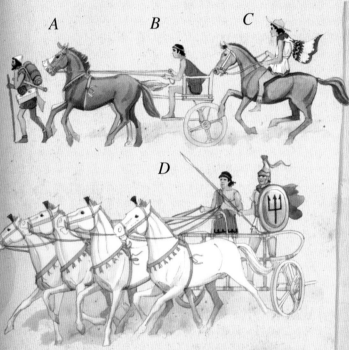

A guide to travelers

Some people that might have traveled on the bumpy Greek roads could include:

• A: An army porter, carrying food, tools, and equipment.

• B: A rich man's groom, driving his master's two-horse cart.

• C: A young traveler, riding a fast, well-bred horse.

• D: An army officer and driver, in a four-horse war chariot.

Journeys by road

Narrow mountain passes were for walkers or sure-footed mules. Better paths ran along the coast in eastern Greece where the mountains sloped gently down to the sea. They were built for wheeled traffic: fast chariots or lumbering farm carts stacked with huge clay jars of grain.

In 490 BC, during the Persian Wars, a messenger ran 26 miles (42 km) from the plains of Marathon to Athens to announce an Athenian victory.

The first marathon

huff! puff!

No 4

Politics and voting

At a trial, each juror was given two metal discs (ballots). The one with the hollow center meant "guilty," the other one "not guilty."

The earliest city-states were ruled by warlords or (in the case of Sparta) kings. In the 6th century BC, many tyrants—strong men discontented with old-style government—seized power. Other states were ruled by oligarchs, who were unelected, wealthy men.

Suicide of Socrates

Socrates was a famous philosopher and an inspiring teacher. But he lived at a time of political unrest, and the government accused him of "corrupting the young." He was condemned to death. In fact, Socrates had not wanted to break the law. He had simply hoped to teach his students how to tell good government from bad. To show his respect for the rule of the law, he agreed to commit suicide by drinking poison in 399 BC.

New democracy

In the 5th century BC, a new form of democratic government developed. All important decisions were made at public assemblies. Any adult male citizen could attend, make speeches, and vote.

Be prepared!
Always expect the very worst

The assembly in Athens met every nine days. About 5000 citizens attended. Meetings were often noisy and argumentative.

Who couldn't vote?

- Women were not allowed to vote or take part in government.

- Foreigners had no rights to vote, even if they had been living in Greece for many years.

- Slaves were never treated equally with free citizens, so they could not vote.

- As a punishment for bad behavior, criminals lost many civil rights, including the right to vote.

Political life

Government leaders were chosen by citizens voting at public elections. Athenians also voted in criminal trials. Verdicts were based on majority votes. Citizens could also punish bad politicians by voting to banish ("ostracize") them for 10 years.

The Council House (bouleuterion).

No 3

The Olympic Games

The Olympic Games were very important to the ancient Greeks, so important that even wars were halted to let the sports festival take place. However, the events needed a lot of training and were often so dangerous that they resulted in serious injury and sometimes death!

Watch out!

Though the competition was a religious event, not all the spectators were honorable. The large crowds attracted all sorts of undesirable characters.

Pancratium

Just about anything goes in this event. It was a mixture of boxing and wrestling. Competitors were allowed to choke and punch each other, even when they were on the floor. Fighters were known to have died from their injuries. However, it was forbidden to kill opponents in the wrestling or boxing matches, either deliberately or accidentally.

Thump!

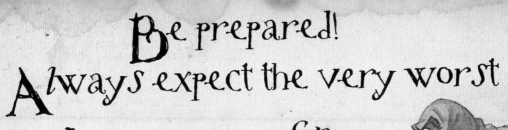

Be prepared!
Always expect the very worst

It's a knockout!

Grrrr!

Boxers were terrifying to look at. They wore leather padding on their hands; some had metal studs to inflict extra pain on their opponents. There was no allowance made for differences in opponents' sizes.

eeek!

Obeying the rules

Every contest was watched closely by referees to make sure that no one was cheating. Athletes who cheated could be disqualified, or they might have to pay a fine to the Olympic committee. The worst crime of all was bribing a referee or an opponent.

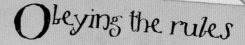

On horseback

Chariot races were seen as good practice for war. Up to 40 chariots took part in a single race, so the sport was very dangerous. At the turning posts, the chariots often got tangled up. Collisions were common and accidents and injuries ranged from minor sprains to broken bones and even death.

Someone loosened my bolts!!

No 2

Spartans at war

Greek city-states were rivals, and were often at war. There were also defensive wars against foreign enemies, especially Persia. Within city-states, civil unrest broke out between rich and poor, opposing political parties, or masters and slaves.

It was the duty of the Greek citizens to fight to defend their homeland.

The Persian wars

In the 6th century BC, the Persians were carving out an empire for themselves. They sparked a series of clashes with the Greek city-states, which lasted over 50 years. Persian armies fought with bows and arrows, short spears, and daggers. The elite Persian army was called "immortal" because it was kept at a constant strength of 10,000 men.

Be prepared!
Always expect the very worst

Men in training had to go on long marches and learn to throw spears.

"You call yourself real men?!"

City-state rivalries

War broke out between the city-states of Sparta and Athens. During the Persian Wars, the Spartans and Athenians fought together to defend Greece, but the two could not be more different. Athens was a center of culture and learning, whereas Sparta was a military state where the majority of people were slaves and all the male citizens were soldiers.

Spartan soldiers

Spartan children were not treated well. Their childhood was meant to prepare them for the harshness of later life and military service. Discipline was tough. They were taught to jeer at the weak, and learned how to be cunning; they were taught to steal, even taking holy food from temples.

Military service

At the age of 18, Greek men became *ephebes*. This meant they were ready to become citizens, but first they had to prove themselves worthy. Ephebes had to live by strict rules for two years, including a period of compulsory military service.
Learning to be a soldier was tough.

No 1

Life as a slave

Without slaves, the Greeks would have had no time for art or scholarship. Slaves made up a quarter of the population in many Greek cities. Although they were surrounded by a brilliant civilization, slaves' lives were often very grim.

Captured!

Slave traders trapped people and sold them as slaves. They also bought prisoners from warlords who had captured enemies in battle, and children from poor families who could not afford to feed them.

Traders took the slaves to the slave market in the agora (marketplace).

28

Be prepared!
Always expect the very worst

Punishments

- If slaves ran away, they would be brought back in chains.

- Slaves were beaten if their owner got angry. Few slaves were actually beaten to death, because they cost too much to replace.

- If owners no longer trusted their slaves, they could sell them to whoever offered the best price.

- Male slaves could be sent to work in the deep, dark silver mines, where the heat was stifling and the air was full of poisonous fumes.

Lowest of the low

Slaves were the lowest-ranking people in Greece. They were thought of as objects, with no human dignity at all. Slaves couldn't vote, serve on juries, or debate government plans. They also couldn't take time off, rest if they were ill, or leave their workplace.

It's all over!

If a slave dropped dead from exhaustion, they were buried where they fell. A simple burial was the best most slaves could hope for. They would be laid in an unmarked grave, with no funeral ceremonies or prayers.

Smash!

Haul away!

29

Glossary

Abacus A frame with three rows of beads, used as a calculating machine.

Agora Open space for holding a town market and doing business.

Altar Table or slab of stone, placed outside Greek temples, where sacrifices to the gods were made.

Anesthetic A drug which causes numbness in the body or a loss of consciousness.

Assembly The main decision-making body in Athens. It met to discuss government plans. It also appointed officials to run the city.

Athlete A term from the Greek meaning "one who competes."

Ballot Small metal or pottery token, about the size of a pebble, used when voting.

Barbarian Anyone who was not a Greek. The Greeks believed that all barbarians were uncivilized.

Bouleuterion Council house where a town's officials met.

Citizen Adult male who lived in a city-state and had the right to take part in political decision-making at the assembly.

City-state A self-governing city and the surrounding land.

Civilization A society with its own laws, customs, beliefs, and artistic traditions.

Colony Territory ruled by people from another country.

Democracy A society where all citizens can have a say, or vote, in the way that the society operates.

Drachma A common Greek coin. In the late 5th century BC, one drachma was the average wage for a skilled day's work.

Ephebe Young man aged between 15 and 20 who might be called up for military service.

Ex-voto An offering of thanks (usually in the shape of a body part) hung up in a temple and dedicated to the god of healing.

Immortal Able to live forever.

Juror Member of the public who attends a trial in a law court to decide whether the accused person is guilty of the crime.

Kottabos Game (throwing wine at a target) played at symposia (dinner parties).

Lyre Musical instrument sometimes made from a tortoise shell.

Mount Olympus Mountain in northern Greece. Home of the Greek gods and goddesses.

Offerings Goods given to gods and goddesses to ask for help or give thanks for blessings.

Oiketai Household slaves.

Oligarchs Rich male rulers.

Ostracize To punish by sending someone away from their homeland for ten years.

Pancratium A brutal sport which was a mixture of boxing and wrestling, with few rules to prevent serious injury.

Persia The huge empire which covered much of the area east of Greece, c. 550 BC–350 BC.

Philosophers Scholars who study the world around them and discuss the best way to live. Many ancient Greek philosophers' writings are still read today.

Phoenicians People who lived in modern Lebanon and the neighboring lands from around 1100 BC to 300 BC.

Sacrifice An offering, usually an animal or special food, given to the gods in the hope of winning their favor or averting their anger.

Slaves Men, women, and children who are not free, but are owned by other people.

Sparta The second most prominent city-state in 5th century BC Greece, famed for its emphasis on a strict military life.

Stylus A pointed stick used for inscribing letters on a wax tablet.

Symposium (plural **symposia**) A dinner party for men, sometimes for serious discussions, other times for drunken entertainment.

Index

A
altar 18
assembly 23

B
ballots 22
barbarians 9
boxing 25

C
chariots 21, 25
children 12–13, 27, 28
city-states 7, 22, 27
crafts 9
craftworkers 9, 18–19

D
democracy 22
doctors 14–15

E
education 8, 13
exports 11

F
family 12–13
farm 16–17
food 10–11

G
gods 6, 15, 18
grain 11, 21
grapes 10, 17

H
Hippocrates 14
houses 18–19

I
imports 11

K
kottabos 11

L
landscape 7
language 9

M
Marathon 21
marriage 12
medicine 14–15
military 27
Mount Olympus 6

O
offerings 15
oiketai 19
oligarchs 22
olives 10, 17
Olympic games 24–25

P
pancratium 24
Persia 21, 26–27
Phoenician language 9
politics 22–23
population 19, 28
pottery 9
punishments 15, 23, 29

R
religion 6
roads 21

S
ships 20
slaves 12, 16, 17, 19, 23,
        26, 27, 29
Socrates 22
Spartans 26–27
storms 20
streets 19
surgical instruments 14
symposium 10

T
trade 11
travel 20–21
travelers 21

V
voting 23

W
water 10, 20
wildlife 7
wine 10–11, 17
women 8, 10, 12, 18, 23